Secrets of Retail Real Estate: How Successful Retailers Win

Steve Morris

Copyright © 2019 Steve Morris

All rights reserved.

ISBN: 9781712109878

Except where otherwise provided in the text of this publication and except as provided by law, no portion of this publication may be reproduced, copied, stored in a retrieval system, or transmitted in any form or by any means, electronic, mechanical, photocopying, recording, or otherwise, without express written permission of the publisher.

CONTENTS

Acknowledgements i
Preface 1
The Current State of Retail Real Estate 4
Managing Risk and Avoiding Unforced Errors 8
Start with the Customer 11
Strategic Framework 16
Store Model 18
Market Planning 23
Portfolio Planning 27
Multiply Options 34
The Truth about Sales Models 36
Review, Refresh 38
Real Estate Communications 40
Communication that Works 42
    Deal Flow 42
    Negotiating Leverage and Shareholder Value 42
Lease Language and Letter of Intent 46
Store Prototype 50
Market Rent 52
Managing Landlords 55
Real Estate Executive Committee Meeting 58
    The Deal Pre-Meeting 58
    The Deal Meeting 59
    Best Practice 59
    Build a Real Estate Package that Performs 60
Corporate Finance Considerations:
    Capital and Depreciation 62
    Tenant Allowance 64
    Leverage 67
Pro Forma: What It Counts, What It Misses 69
Conclusion 71
About the Author 74

ACKNOWLEDGMENTS

The author would like to thank Adam Morris for the cover artwork and illustrations that appear throughout this book, as well as the many colleagues who have read and helped edit this book, and more importantly who contributed to my learnings over the years. I would also like to thank David and Shadra Bruce for their editing, proofreading, and publishing services. The publication of this book would not have been possible without their assistance and expertise.

PREFACE

This is a real estate primer for C-suite executives who are new to real estate.

Now a C-level retail executive, you have successfully climbed the steep corporate ladder and are responsible for approving real estate investments. Your "learning process" is the monthly real estate committee meetings; for medium- to larger-sized programs, this committee meets roughly two hours a month, ten times a year – a total of twenty hours representing less than one percent of annual work life. Deals are approved following five minutes of discussion. Other than the enthusiasm of the presenter, there is little to distinguish good from bad.

This book is for you.

You started life as an ecommerce brand, disdaining physical stores, and now face the reality that customers like you better if you have a brick-and-mortar presence. You have also discovered, at some inflection point, that the cost of acquiring new customers exceeds their lifetime value. Brick-and-mortar stores have become the lowest cost alternative to acquiring customers and growing your brand. While you possess big data and machine learning skill sets from which to leverage, and the tremendous advantage of talking directly to your customers every day, you have no internal learnings on how to profitably operate a retail store, much less how to acquire the right real estate at the right price.

This book is for you.

You are a wholesale brand with no direct connection to your end customer, and your distribution channels guard their data like Fort Knox. You know how to build brands and have tremendous brand awareness but have neither the data skill sets of the digitally native brands nor the retail operation skill sets of established retailers. It's the twenty-first century, where data is king and where brand customers want to buy products anytime, anywhere, thereby forcing the need to build a store channel.

This book is for you.

You are a private equity or venture capital investor. Retail ranks right up there with technology as a creator of wealth, and you are investing in start-up and mature retailers alike. For a financial investor, the single biggest leverage point (after talent) is making critical capital allocation decisions, and real estate dominates the capital investment budgets of all retailers.

This book is for you.

Real estate is specialty retail's largest asset, largest liability, largest use of capital, and largest expense category. Real estate decisions, even for moderate-size chains, commit tens of millions of dollars in capital and future lease obligations. Great real estate can significantly leverage results and poor real estate choices can derail all other best efforts.

I have worked with over 100 retailers that have smart and dedicated real estate teams, and they all have unique and smart approaches to managing real estate. Yet we often find management is uncertain if they are getting the best results or making the best decisions.

Real estate is often described as a silo function but, in reality, it is an island. It operates on an entirely different time frame from the rest of the company – deals can be 6 to 18 months in the making. CEOs, CFOs, merchants, and store operators often live by the daily comp sales results. Real estate is in another time zone entirely, with a "launch it and leave it" mentality. A bad real estate decision is painful to real estate and no doubt leaves a scar on their psyche, but by the time a store opens and posts poor results, it is 18 months in their rearview mirror. A bad real estate decision for store operations never leaves a scar – it's an open wound for ten years. They launch it and live with it.

Silo or island, the fact remains that there is often a disconnect between real estate and the rest of the company, and there is often dissatisfaction with the results. Improving real estate results means understanding and improving the myriad processes involved. As the US auto industry painfully learned from the Japanese, quality doesn't occur by inspecting the finished product (i.e. the real estate approval meeting); it occurs downstream by fixing processes.

This book aims to connect the dots and help company management develop, invest in, and structure better real estate business processes, better analytics, and more structured strategies – to better understand the real estate you own and might own, and maximize the return from your real estate investments and achieve better results.

Consider this a guide on how to create guard rails to ensure deals meet long-term market growth, asset management, and financial objectives.

1

THE CURRENT STATE OF RETAIL REAL ESTATE

In 1983, John Naisbitt's highly influential business book, Megatrends: Ten New Directions Transforming Our Lives, had become a best seller and corporate America enthusiastically adopted its premise: Strategically anticipating future trends was the ultimate key to business success. At that point in time, Dayton-Hudson Corporation, the parent company of Target, Dayton's, Hudson's, John A. Brown, Diamond's, B. Dalton Bookseller, Lechmere, and Dayton-Hudson Jewelers, was the nation's fifth-largest general merchandise retailer behind Kmart, Sears, JCPenney, and Federated, and just ahead of Walmart. If knowing the future was the key to success, the board of directors wanted a "crystal ball" glimpse.

Among the many bromides, including the increasing importance of Hispanics and other ethnicities, the impact of women in the workplace, and the importance that consumers were placing on information, was the bold prediction that retail square footage growth and construction would soon end.

It was easy to predict brick-and-mortar growth was coming to an end. The US had far more retail square footage than that of any other nation: ten feet per person in the US compared to two or three feet per capita in Europe. Kmart had expanded nationally, and every market had at least one other regional discount department store chain (Walmart, Target, and another dozen nameplates). There were about 600 malls, each within 20 minutes of over 80% of the population. The malls were not only anchored by Sears and JCPenney, but also by two other competing local fashion department stores, and these malls were populated by a hundred vibrant specialty stores representing virtually every merchandise category, from shoes to toys to housewares to every slice of fashion apparel.

Yet, incredibly, in the next 20 years, retail space doubled and then doubled again.

The regional mall world continued to grow, peaking at 1,220 centers. Competing real estate and retail concepts also exploded. Big-box specialty store growth likewise flourished. In 1983, only Toys "R" Us had a national footprint. Over the next two decades, with ample investor money and developer resources, specialty category after specialty category became big-box opportunities. Home Depot, with fewer than 100 stores in 1983, became a national chain, followed by Lowes. Office Depot and Staples emerged in office supplies, absorbing copycats along the way. Borders fought Barnes & Noble for market dominance across the country, often opening across the street from each other. Circuit City became the first national electronics chain, only to fade and be replaced by Best Buy. Bed Bath & Beyond, Party City, DSW, David's Bridal, and DICK's Sporting Goods emerged in their respective categories. Even things you put things into had its own venue in The Container Store. Fifteen hundred power centers were added to retail space inventory.

Strip center developments seemed to pop up on every corner, populated by some 9,000 Blockbusters, 5,000 Radio Shacks, 25,000 Dollar Stores, and 5,000-plus fashion discount stores under Stein Mart, Cato Fashions, TJ Maxx, Marshalls, and Ross Stores nameplates. Outlet centers serving cash-strapped middle-income families became the most profitable real estate location for both the retailers that launched a value version of their brand and the developers that built them.

The hugely successful Easton Town Center, in Columbus OH, spawned about 400 wannabe lifestyle centers, none quite as successful as the original.

We have now come full circle.

The number of regional shopping centers have now shrunk by a third. The fashion department store chains that anchored those centers have merged. The once iconic name plates of Lazarus,

Marshall Field's, Burdines, Dayton's and Hudson's are now consolidated under the Macy's badge. Sears has become overleveraged and irrelevant, closing stores and selling its real estate at a rapid pace. JC Penney is likewise retrenching after a disastrous attempt to shed its reliance on weekly promotions. Regional mall market share has waned, and now retailers are reporting significant traffic declines in even some top-tier centers.

The dozen regional discount store chains are long gone, as is, for all practical purposes Kmart. All that remain are Walmart and Target. Outlet center growth has peaked and is downtrending. Private equity did the big-box industry no service, adding enormous debt which has hamstrung many otherwise viable retail brands, including, most recently, Toys "R" Us.

Amazon is now a dominant retailer across nearly all categories and has elevated convenience to equal importance as the traditional price and quality determinants as a definition of value. A host of digitally native brands have followed in Amazon's wake. They are well funded and have seemingly no imperative to prioritize profitability over growth and market share.

The shopper today is wildly different from yesterday, embracing technology and using mobile, social media, and web-based tools as an integral part of shopping. We have all embraced the convenience of wanting it when we want it, delivered where we want it. Clearly, legacy customer-engagement models no longer work.

The traditional retail economic model is under siege. Total retail sales continue to grow at about the rate of GDP growth. But the expense of delivering great customer experience, from labor costs to construction costs, to an additional omnichannel cost layer, is growing faster. A favorable cost-of-goods cycle achieved through offshoring is coming to an end with the recent tariff wars reversing. Retail profits are being squeezed, putting additional pressure on managing occupancy expense, typically along with store labor, a number-one- or number-two-expense category in specialty retail.

With the growing importance of ecommerce, brutal competition, over-leveraging, shifting customer expectations, and perhaps just too darn much retail space per capita, the retail store landscape is transforming rapidly.

But it is also safe to say that brick-and-mortar retail it is not going away. Pure play ecommerce brands quickly learned their customers demand an in-store option. Kate Hudson is evolving her successful Fabletics ecommerce brand with the announced plan to open 75 new stores. Amazon, whose early model decimated the book retail business, is, ironically, opening bookstores and has recently bought Whole Foods to obtain, overnight, a national brick-and-mortar footprint. Pure play ecommerce models do not maximize sales; customers want omnichannel.

Traditional real estate strategies are not the answer. The "new to brick-and-mortar retail" concepts generally eschew the perceived mass-merchant connotation of traditional shopping centers and are joining innovators, such as Lululemon and Vineyard Vines, in finding alternative locations, spurring high street and community center retail development. The economy has not been a friend to the middle-class shoppers that drove the prior rapid expansion of suburban shopping centers. The aging Baby Boom generation has been supplanted by Millennials and Gen Zers who find alternative urban and community centers more appealing than the traditional suburban enclosed mall. Shopping centers are no longer the safe bet for retail expansion.

The new environment is moving fast, and its impact is far from settled. But one thing is clear: It plainly raises the stakes regarding brick-and-mortar investment decisions.

2

MANAGING RISK AND AVOIDING UNFORCED ERRORS

Two themes will recur throughout this book: avoidable errors and risk management.

Avoidable Errors

Former professional basketball player Chris Webber famously called for a time out with 11 seconds remaining in the 1993 NCAA championship game and the Wolverines trailing the Tar Heels by two points. With no time outs remaining for Michigan, the penalty resulted in a change* of possession and a lost opportunity to tie the game.

Such gaffes are now called "avoidable errors." Coaches call them teachable moments.

Sadly, avoidable errors are not limited to high-profile athletes. According to a John Hopkins study, avoidable medical errors result in 250,000 patient deaths and are the third leading cause of death in the US.

Real estate portfolios are replete with avoidable errors:

- Over-stored markets
- Picking the wrong location
- Overlapping trade areas, resulting in two average or mediocre stores instead of one good one
- Wasteful capital spending on suboptimal aging stores

- Long-term renewals in declining centers
- Over-reliance on a single store model, limiting real estate alternatives
- Poor corporate communications that hamstring or derail deal negotiators
- Lack of disciplined financial approval thresholds, allowing approval of suboptimal deals, or conversely, overly conservative and inflexible approval criteria, leaving opportunities on the table
- Inflexible growth plans, ignoring opportunities and risks of current leasing environment
- Not understanding the true cost of "free" tenant allowances

These are all correctable process failures. A Walt Kelly saying, coined from the oft-repeated Oliver Hazard Perry quote, resonates throughout this book: "We have met the enemy and he is us." The Real Estate Committee leadership needs to be the coach.

Risk Management

In 2003, Oakland won 103 baseball games with a payroll of $40 million. The Yankees spent $126 million for the same result.

Moneyball, the great Michael Lewis book, detailed how Billy Beane and the Oakland A's developed a winning team despite a seemingly insurmountable obstacle: one of the lowest payrolls in baseball. The A's success was attributed to the intelligent use of statistics to find market inefficiencies in pricing ball players.

Historically, baseball scouts picked players, in part, because "they looked good." That is not unlike how many specialty retailers approach real estate. They "need" to be in South Coast or Aventura or Soho, or on Michigan Avenue or Fifth Avenue or because it "looks" good. "Get me a deal there," is the directive.

Billy Beane didn't bat 1000; he stacked the deck in his favor. If he bought more players with high on-base percentages, the odds were that he would score more runs. He used analytics to improve his opportunity for success.

Billy Beane happened because Bill James and other pioneers developed sabermetrics – rigorous data collected by enthusiasts on every at bat in every situation and then leveraged it to build "smart data" – secondary statistical measures. The old standbys – batting averages and RBIs – were replaced by on-base percentages and slugging averages to measure a player's worth. The "level one" statistics led to more sophisticated, higher-level models, such as WAR (wins above replacement) and VORP (value over replacement player), which have become the arsenal for both armchair and real general managers throughout the league.

Retail analytics is much more complicated than baseball, and unlike baseball, there are no authenticated, published sabermetrics for real estate. There is scant published statistical data on shopping center performance. Most competitor and center performance data retailers glean comes from developers touting their properties.

But even imperfect data is better than a "looks good" metric, and well-structured analytics can help rank opportunities and improve the probability of success. Lack of disciplined analytics is the cause of many of the unforced errors mentioned above. In the last 30 years, the cost of analytics has dropped tenfold. Given that real estate is the dominant use of capital (lease obligations are the largest balance sheet liability, and occupancy expense is often the largest expense category), there is really no reason not to spend a modest amount of money to improve real estate selection and portfolio strategy.

Can analytics improve the odds of success and eliminate unforced errors? Absolutely – if structured correctly.

3

START WITH THE CUSTOMER

B. Dalton Bookseller was founded by Bruce Dayton, one of five Dayton brothers of Dayton's Department Store and Dayton-Hudson Corporation (now Target) fame. He is rumored to have named the bookstore after himself with the slight substitution of the L for the T due to midwestern humility. B. Dalton began life just as the explosion of regional mall development occurred, and it became the first and the largest national bookstore chain, peaking at 798 stores in 1986 with virtually all of its stores positioned in suburban malls. When asked why it was successful, his reply was simple: "We put books where people are."

In the heydays of the 1960s and 1970s suburban growth, and with the rapid expansion of regional malls as shopping destinations, that was good strategy. That strategy stopped working effectively around the time B. Dalton hit its peak store count. Dayton Hudson saw the end of its growth coming and divested from B. Dalton in 1987.

Today, putting stores "where people are" is much more complicated. The suburban baby boom generation has been supplanted by Millennials' more eclectic lifestyle choices, including preferences for experiences, lower brand loyalty, and willingness to shop everywhere – from traditional malls and department stores to high street boutiques, power, lifestyle, and outlet centers to thrift stores and, of course, online.

Additionally, the internet, ecommerce, and mobile have completely changed how customers engage with the brands they love. Putting a store where your customer is now must include a digital presence.

But the core principals of successful real estate remain the same. You need to define your core customer, understand how many customers you need to make your store model work, and understand how far they travel, which determines how many stores you need for market coverage: Who, How Many, How Far.

Who

Kate grew up on a farm in the Midwest, studied biology in college, and opened a store to sell homemade, natural beauty products. Her down-to-earth, solid Midwest values were the foundation on which Bath & Body Works, one the great retail success stories of the last two decades, was built. She was fiercely protective of the brand, demanding its stores be stocked with wholesome natural products.

Of course, Kate is a completely fictional brand persona. Brand descriptors and brand personas are useful. They certainly help define the type of shopping centers and the type of neighbors a brand would like to be near. But "customer" must be accurately defined statistically to be useful in the analytics of real estate planning.

"Who shops us" is determined by broad but measurable demographic and psychographic descriptors. Psychographics are demographics combined with behavior. Demographics may define your customer as college educated with family income over $100,000. But consider two individuals who have advanced college degrees and earn $100,000, but one drives a pickup truck, hunts, and buys season tickets to the local football team while the other drives a Volvo, reads Architectural Digest and buys season tickets to the local symphony. While they look the same in broad stroke demographic variables, it is unlikely that both are your customers.

The marketing geniuses serving consumer brands developed lifestyle segmentation techniques decades ago to capture these differences, and most real estate market research companies license that data and can append lifestyle segments to customer records based on latitude and longitude coordinates. Claritas PRIZM, Mosaic® by Experian, and ESRI Tapestry are the best-known geodemographic segmentation systems, and all three cluster households in about 70 unique lifestyle segments based on similar income, education, occupation, and spending attributes. Across our research clients, we find that typically 12 to 18 out of those 70 segments account for 70% of sales. It is a useful way to quantify "who."

More recently, the explosion of mobile and social data is leading to a new way of defining customers by directly tracking their journeys and social media likes. Where a large retailer may have millions of customer transactions in the loyalty card or CRM platform, mobile and social data are measured on hundreds of millions of data points and require machine learning and AI to aggregate and interpret the massive data points effectively.

How Many

In October 2007, a specialty lifestyle center called Hill Country Galleria opened in Bee Cave, Texas, on the western outskirts of Austin. The shopping center got an early commitment to add Abercrombie & Fitch to the lease plan when the brand was peaking as the iconic teen and young adult fashion retailer. Tenant A begets tenant B – if A can go there, surely B can go there – just because. Soon, the center had a pretty good lineup of prospective brands, followed by signed leases, followed by a grand opening.

The Galleria filed for bankruptcy protection in May of 2009.

Evidently, neither the developer nor the lenders nor any of the specialty retailers scrambling to open stores in Bee Cave, Texas checked to see if anyone lived within 15 miles of Bee Cave, and the great recession of 2008 halted any potential housing growth that might have averted the situation.

The center emerged from bankruptcy, changed ownership, recalibrated its rents, turned over its small shop space, and added a grocery and cinema anchor. It recently celebrated its tenth anniversary. Perhaps Austin's growth has caught up, and Hill Country can now support small shop fashion tenants, but that is no solace to the retailers who spent millions opening and then closing stores.

Bee Cave is hardly an isolated example. I worked in Hunt Valley, Maryland on a corporate restructuring project shortly before becoming the CFO of Limited Brands, Inc. Real Estate Group where I was hired to "fix" real estate. Limited had twelve brands at the time and six had stores in Hunt Valley. All were in

Secrets of Retail Real Estate: How Successful Retailers Win

the bottom 5% of performance.

Hunt Valley is just north of Baltimore and was developed by the Rouse Company, a highly respected Baltimore-based developer. The Rouse Company simply did not make mistakes. They built great properties, communities, and shopping centers. Based on their reputation alone, Hunt Valley leased up quickly. No one checked into the location. Hunt Valley was horse country with minimum lot sizes of five acres – very rich horse country to be sure. So, it might have met the "who" criteria, but a few rich horse breeders and hunt clubs were not going to drive enough business to sustain a mall full of moderate brands whose trade area overlapped with a highly successful Towson Town Center.

In both Hill Country and Hunt Valley, developers and retailers forgot about the question of "how many." Research analysts, however, have now developed a shorthand methodology to calculate "how many." If an established retailer plotted all their customers in Boston, it would likely indicate their core customers come from every corner of the city, from wealthy Beacon Street in Back Bay to more moderate Somerville neighborhoods. But using the entire metropolitan area of Boston to answer the question of how many is not statistically useful. Hence, we talk in terms of primary trade areas, or what the Europeans much more descriptively call "catchment" areas.

There are various technical methodologies used to create these boundaries; three- or five-mile rings are common but not very accurate. With the advent of desktop GIS tools, most demographers can easily calculate drive-time trade areas. Our company developed an algorithm that measures penetration by block group using actual customer information. We have found this algorithm gives us good results when we do higher-level statistical modeling. The end result of any of these methods is a tight amoeba-shaped trade area boundary that represents 60% to 70% of a brands' sales. Demographic and psychographic tables can then be calculated to identify the "how many" core customers are required to support a store.

How Far

"How far" is closely related to trade areas. Existing customer data or mobility data can be used to definitively calculate primary trade areas for existing stores. For new stores, and for transfer or recapture analysis, you need to know how far customers travel to estimate a trade area.

Every brand's trade area is different. Cabela's can comfortably build a store, seemingly in the middle of nowhere, and measure trade areas in hundreds of miles, confident its loyal hunting and fishing fans will travel hours to shop; indeed, some customers camp overnight. An upscale department store may need 100,000 households with a median household income over $125,000 living within a 20-minute drive of the store. Neighborhood pizza restaurants must rely on population density within five or ten minutes.

PROCESS

For existing brick-and-mortar retailers, start with your customer data. Use customer data to build trade areas for your existing stores, using available GIS tools. Build a statistical model of customer attributes (who, how many, how far) within those trade areas. This is the first, simplest, and most cost-effective investment to benchmark real estate opportunities. As the lessons of Hunt Valley and Hill Country Galleria demonstrate, it is an immediate and cost-effective means to eliminate one type of unforced error. Once trade areas and customer data points are mapped, use them as a baseline starting point for analysis.

For companies new to brick-and-mortar retail, pattern trade-area reach after like competitors and build trade areas using drive time software. Use the resulting customer demographics to rank opportunities. Revisit and refine these assumptions as the store opening program matures and as real customer data becomes available.

4

STRATEGIC FRAMEWORK

Who, how many, and how far are level-one analytics and great data points. But analytics is a raw material – the nails and lumber of a real state strategy. Retailers need to build the structure. Like the Amish barn raising, real estate needs to pour the foundation, square up the building, and build the framework.

The three legs of real estate strategy are: store model, market planning, and portfolio planning

Store model is our shorthand for the real estate portion of your operating model. It defines size, productivity, capital investment, customer psychographics and demographics, center types, desirable neighbors, visibility, access, and other real estate attributes that combine to make a maximize profitably the brick-and-mortar strategy.

For existing retailers, a backward-looking analysis of what works best validates the store model. For new-to-brick-and-mortar retailers, it is a plan, or hypothesis, of what will work, to be tested and refined.

Market planning, often overlooked by deal approval committees, will eliminate many unforced errors. Retailers need to plan for success among a myriad of choices for real estate – from high streets and regional malls to grocery anchored community centers and outlets, to name a few. Understanding the nuances of each market, and where your prospective customers live and work, is an essential step.

Portfolio planning, also called portfolio optimization, portfolio strategy, or asset management, is a proven process for optimizing performance and capital investment, applied to existing real estate. Applying sound asset management principals to the strategic management of the real estate portfolio will improve performance and return on investment.

While real estate is execution-focused and ultimately opportunistic (no one gets 100% of their strategic objectives accomplished, as it takes two to tango), success increases exponentially when it is executed within a clearly understood store model with priorities that have been established through market and portfolio planning..

5

STORE MODEL

There are hundreds of thousands of retail store nameplates. A simple Google search of "retail stores Columbus Ohio" generates over ten thousand results. In terms of barriers to entry, retail is one of the easiest industries in which to launch a business. Every industry segment imaginable has a convention or trade show to connect store owners with everything they need to operate a store, and all possible vendors to fill a store with attractive merchandise.

Need a point of sale system with software to track merchandise sales by SKU and collect customer names and track behavior? It's available, easy to configure, and compared to two decades ago, inexpensive. Want to launch an educational toy store? Go to US or German or Japanese toy fairs and see in one place everything new coming to market. Meet the companies directly or work with a wholesaler to pick a line and arrange shipping and financing.

Today, the internet is making these connections so much simpler. A friend of mine who runs a small accessory store can peruse online catalogs, make online payments using PayPal, and have the latest assortments shipped from Asia and displayed in his store in as little as seven days.

With such a low barrier to entry for retail, many try, but few succeed. There are only a relatively small handful of retailers with national or potential national footprints – perhaps 250 chains that operate over 100 stores in multiple markets. To be sure there is constant turnover. Retail is a dog-eat-dog world and highly competitive. Every year there is a new bankruptcy and a handful of exciting new concepts emerging to step into the national spotlight.

But that just underscores the difficulty of engineering what we will call a successful operating model – an integrated combination of merchandising, branding, supply chain, digital, retail, customer engagement, and real estate strategies. We call the real estate portion of this complex infrastructure the "store model."

The store model drives real estate site selection. It defines the who, how many, and how far, as well as store design, store size, store construction costs, center types and desirable co-tenancy. Real estate strategy can't exist without a well-defined store model.

Successful operating models have led to enormous fortunes. The Walton (Walmart) family fortune, is collectively one of the greatest fortunes ever amassed in the history or the world. Les Wexner, founder of L Brands; the Fishers, founders of Gap; and their savant, Mickey Drexler, are modern icons who have created multiple retail concepts and became billionaires in the process. They follow in the footsteps of Sears, Lazarus, and the Daytons, who all created retail empires. Amancio Ortega, founder of Inditex, is today's genius, with a fortune estimated at $70 billion, making him Europe's second-richest person behind Bernard Arnault, Chairman and CEO of Louis Vuitton. All of them developed highly productive operating models which, once designed and perfected, were rolled out and replicated through brick-and-mortar expansions.

The Limited, in its original form, was the highest return stock on the NYSE between 1975 and 1990. An investment of $1,000 at the beginning of that run was worth $60 million at its peak in 2016, beating the investments of Warren Buffet, GE, and every other US stock. Their store model worked almost everywhere. The ecosystem Wexner built included a strategic acquisition of Mast industries in 1970, making the owners of Mast 20% owners of The Limited. But Mast gave Wexner the early capacity to exploit a fast-to-market strategy. Unlike today's "fast fashion," with short production runs and ever-changing assortments, The Limited made big bets on key items – "limited" assortments. By identifying fashion items early during European trips, interpreting them for the US market, and then sourcing through Mast, The Limited was the "hot" fashion store for more than a decade. The Limited understood early on that in a brick-and-mortar world dominated by regional malls, your store window and the first 10 feet of visibility was your billboard, which would drive customers across the threshold – and they worked hard at delivering that week after week.

Real estate was part of the store model as well, and that decade conveniently saw the explosion of the suburban enclosed mall development, which was a ready-made growth strategy that The Limited and other specialty retailers benefitted from. Stores were appropriately sized, rents and labor costs were reasonable (cheap by today's metrics), and they had great teams to execute deals and build stores as fast as developers could build malls. Through acquisitions (Victoria's Secret, Lerner New York, Lane Bryant) and internal start-ups (Express, Bath & Body Works), The Limited diversified and leveraged that real estate environment to grow and reinvent itself long past the nadir of The Limited stores' dominance.

The Gap became the model specialty retailer of the 1990s. They had many of the same elements as other specialty retailers of the time, selling basic denim and t-shirts. But (as an observer from the sidelines) what seemed to set them apart in that era was their total ownership of color. They did an incredible job of managing a coordinated color palette across their merchandise and transitioning the color story from month to month, season to season. It helped them become the dominant retailer of an era that embraced basics as a fashion necessity. Gap then conceived Old Navy, with an entirely different store (and real estate) model. Old Navy was designed as a big-box, off-mall, value-priced vertical-fashion family apparel store. As Old Navy reached critical mass, they adapted by buying mass market advertising to drive customers to stores.

The discount department store industry is a fascinating story of competing operating models. Today, with only Target and Walmart surviving, it's hard to remember that there were once dozens of discount department stores all trying to capitalize on the early success or Kmart. Kmart's operational store model was very successful – they expanded rapidly through build-to-suit deals, pushed the value message relentlessly through in-store signing, "Blue light Specials," and weekly circulars.

Target originated as a high-low discounter with higher fashion and higher quality content than Kmart was willing to carry. Target's operating strategy was simply: get customers in the store on a weekly basis and fill their shopping carts. The former was accomplished with weekly circulars of advertised specials and the latter by developing a race-track store design with the weekly advertised specials prominently displayed on end caps. The customer pushed the cart around the store, not only buying the weekly specials but filling the cart along the way. It was a very effective strategy, but the cost of weekly circulars required Target to carefully plan and enter markets with a critical mass of stores. This confined their growth to sizable metro markets.

Walmart, in contrast, did not engage in high-low pricing, weekly circulars, or in-store promotions. Sam Walton was the evangelist of everyday low pricing and relentlessly pursued cost reduction efficiencies and pushed vendors to do the same. The operating mantra was to give Walmart's customers the best deals, every day. They lead the industry in logistics and in adopting cost reduction innovations, a core cultural advantage they exploited in entering the food business. This made their real estate strategy somewhat easier than Target's. In fact, early on they avoided highly competitive metro areas and drove their growth first in small towns in the South, then in urban fringe locations where land was cheap resulting in less overhead and savings that they could pass on to their faithful customers through lower prices.

Every imaginable operating model has success stories. Companies that sell other brands, and thus have a lower gross margin, have a history of success – think Pacific Sunwear in its heyday, or Finish Line or Foot Locker or Sephora today. Operators that have unique and strong branding, allowing high margins also thrive; Abercrombie & Fitch, Victoria's Secret, and Lululemon are notable examples. But aggressive low pricing also works. Fast fashion, with its typically larger store format and incredibly competitive low pricing and product turnover, has created store empires for the likes of H&M, Love Culture, Topshop, Zara, Primark, and Uniqlo.

What do Gap, Victoria's Secret, Lululemon, Warby Parker, Pottery Barn, Kay Jewelers, TJ Maxx, and other easily recognizable names have in common? Not much. If there were a formula, there would be more names on this short list. But through luck, persistence, great merchandising, or great vision, they have all engineered an operating model that is replicable, predictable, and financially successful.

When we work with retailers whose real estate isn't working, what is usually not working is the operating model – that unique collection of attributes that encompass merchandising, marketing, branding, pricing, sourcing, operations, and customer engagement models that drive sales, margin, and profitability. Good real estate cannot fix a bad operating model.

PROCESS

Analyzing existing store performance across a range of variables – geography, center type and size, presence of co-tenants, store age, design type, size of trade area, and more – all help define your store model. This requires building a simple real estate attribute data set, pulling lease data from lease admin, store performance and trends from the accounting system, traffic and conversion data from store operations, center variables and descriptors from real estate, trade area variables from GIS, customer data from CRM (minus personal information), approved deals and deals in process from real estate, store design and age or variables include site ranking, center performance and size, and presence ad performance of key co-tenants.

As brands mature and the real estate environment changes, it is critical to periodically rethink the store model: Who are the customers, how far are they driving, what has ecommerce done to our assumptions, how do our customers cross shop, what is the ideal co-tenancy, what type for retail locations work best for sales and for profitability, and what is our ideal store size? Do we operate multiple formats, and if so, which are the most profitable? Do we perform better with some landlords over others?

Invest in a Business Intelligence ("BI") tool to maintain the data sets, or annually recreate with new customer data and trade areas and then re-examine and refine store model assumptions.

6

MARKET PLANNING

Westfield Citrus Park, previously referred to as Citrus Park Town Center, opened in the Tampa – St. Petersburg – Clearwater Metropolitan area in 1999. It was a beautifully designed mall with super-wide interior aisles and very well leased. The landlord required tenants to build double-high store fronts, and retailers accommodated with innovative design work, making it look like a true two-story streetscape. By look and design, it should have emerged as a dominant class-A mall. It never reached that potential. The Tampa Bay area was perhaps the most overdeveloped major market in the country. If a retailer graded Tampa as a five-store market based on population, there were ten or more shopping center opportunities, and most national specialty retailers opened in all of them with mediocre results.

Real estate market planning began in the department store industry in the early 1960s and subsequently migrated to big-box operators. Sears, JC Penney, Federated, and The May Department Stores Company all had substantial market research departments. Unlike specialty retailers who could merely follow them, the department stores needed to plan markets; their capital investments were too high and leases too long to risk capital without a long-term view of market positioning. In the mid-1980s, Dayton-Hudson, then rolling out Target stores, had a 30-person market research team*. One large, big-box chain that used third-party research was reported to spend $500,000 per market for a market plan. No deal could go to real estate committee without a preceding market plan.

Market planning is about "how many" and "where."

The "how many stores in a market" equation is not rocket science. Using competitor and own-store performance benchmarks, customer data, and market-share data, it is feasible to approximate the number of stores a brand can have nationally and by market within a respectable range. Pittsburgh may grade out to two to three stores, but not six, no matter how many centers are developed. In this era of rapidly evolving center performance and unsettled distribution of online to brick-and-mortar sales, a well-reasoned approach to "how many" stores in a market can prevent overbuilding and oversaturation.

Understanding "where" takes more work and finding the ideal configuration of stores within a market can be complicated. Due to overbuilding or shifting demographics, markets seldom have an ideal configuration of shopping centers. Detroit might pencil as a five-store market, but if you are a mall-based better-fashion concept, there may be only two good opportunities. Cincinnati should be a multi-store market for most moderate and better price-point retailers, but it is dominated by Kenwood Towne Centre, and the second-best opportunity is a small specialty center (Rookwood Commons & Pavilion) in Kenwood's shadow.

Some markets, like Columbus, OH, have totally transformed, with Easton Town Center and Polaris dominating, while Columbus City Center, Northland, Eastland, and Westland malls are closed, closing, scrapped, or heading down that path. Other markets, such as Dayton, OH, should be a one-store market, but sales are fragmented across three ongoing shopping centers. Tucson has two fashion malls within two miles of one another; Louisville has two fashion malls across the street from one another.

Flexibility influences the "where." The traditional shopping center world is in an era of painful realignment: a fourth of the original 1,200 regional malls have closed, and another fourth are likely candidates to close in the future. If real estate opportunities are confined to the regional shopping center world, it may be difficult to pick the winners and losers. An effective strategy for retailers is to maximize their flexibility through multiple store formats that work in alternative locations.

Lululemon can open with a yoga studio as a high street solution or in a neighborhood center. Restoration Hardware can take an iconic building and create its mansion concept. Tommy Bahama can go big with its adjacent restaurant and be on a pad location; vineyard vines can go small with its resort stores. Victoria's Secret can include PINK and Beauty or open separate stores for each brand. Store size and format flexibility provide negotiating power and a better path to optimizing markets.

Good real estate informed by a solid market plan takes patience. Deals come to real estate committee opportunistically, and it isn't uncommon to approve a deal only to realize two years later you should have waited for a space in a better center down the road. Without a roadmap, it is hard to reach your desired destination.

Market plans are essential for portfolio strategy as well. Retailers consistently renew leases in downtrending centers because the deal works, guaranteeing themselves years of negative comp sales. Or they pragmatically accept rent relief to stay in three marginal locations when they should opt to invest and consolidate down to one great space.

From restaurants to dollar stores to high-end luxury brands, market plans are the starting point – advance work that limits the oversaturation, poor positioning, and other costly unforced errors.

PROCESS

Licensing geo-analytic software and household level data can easily cost six figures and hiring internal staff to build the shopping center and competitor data sets required to develop higher-end models can double the data and data analytic costs. Consequently, smaller chains tend to hire third-party market research firms that can spread these costs over multiple clients.

Numerous market research firms can produce market plans with varying degrees of sophistication, optimizing markets based on a household level spend, drive time, and calculated demographics and psychographics within the drive time trade area. The cost of this sophisticated modeling for the 25 top markets is going be less than the $500,000 that big-box companies spent on a single market in the 1990s. This major cost reduction is thanks to the evolution in computer technology which brought computational power to desk GIS systems. For site-agnostic strategies – restaurants, coffee shops, etc. – planning for large scale brick-and-mortar footprints is essential. For brands that perform best with the right neighbors, it is critical to add center quality, attractiveness, and co-tenant variables to the mix. Currently, market research firms are using large mobile data and social data sets, combined with machine learning to generate market and site-specific sale models.

Many specialty retailers that have a handful of stores, even in large metros like Boston or Chicago, use common-sense market planning, informed by mapping existing trade areas and voids, centers, competitors, and customer data points. The real estate teams and store operations add great insights into neighborhoods, centers, and trending developments to identify desirable market opportunities.

Regardless of how a market plan is developed, it is important to prioritize the opportunities in a market. Deals are opportunistic and the number-five opportunity may become available before the number-one. That is important to know. Real estate is in the business of delivering X number of deals, and the company is in the business of making money, so a bird in the hand may well be the best decision. But starting at the bottom in a market can lead to a false impression for both the brand and its customers. Open in a new market in a secondary center and customers will associate you with secondary brands. We naturally overweight recent events, creating a "we opened a store in Memphis and it's below our chain average: therefore, we don't play well in the South" kind of mentality. I've known retailers lament that they were not "West Coast brands," when their problem was that they opened their initial stores in secondary centers. Ranking opportunities in market planning will better manage expectations.

Every deal should come to committee with a market plan and ranking attached, ideally with nearest stores and key competitors highlighted. This constantly validates the market plan, and if the proposed opportunity is at variance, update the plan. It takes five minutes or less of discussion and keeps everyone aligned (See chapter on Real Estate Executive Committee Meeting).

*Much of that head count and expense was simply due to manual tasks. At one point, Dayton-Hudson would go to parking lots and write down license plate numbers, then go to the DMV to look up addresses and get the raw data necessary to build trade areas. Feet-on-the-ground market research was a necessity; there was no easy drive time software that took into account manmade and natural boundaries. Much of that tedious work has now been replaced by GIS (Geographic Information System) technology.

7

PORTFOLIO PLANNING

No parent would outfit one child in Polo and send him or her to an elite private school and then dress a sibling in thrift shop hand-me-downs and enroll him or her in a distressed, crime-ridden public school. Our culture (or perhaps it's simply human nature) has blessed us with an ingrained sense of fairness and equality. One SVP of Store Development expressed the company's remodel or reinvestment program eloquently: "We love all our stores equally. We invest in our brand and no one thinks we have an 'A' brand, a 'B' brand, and a 'C' brand, so all stores get the same treatment."

Unfortunately, for lovers of equality, that philosophy works poorly for retailers when they are charged with improving shareholder returns.

Other than start-ups, every retailer needs a real estate plan that accounts for both new store growth and existing store activity – closings, remodels, repositioning, downsizes, and expansions, which are usually tied to lease expirations or other critical lease dates. These plans, commonly labeled portfolio strategy, feed the annual expense and capital budgeting process as well.

Typically, for mature retailers, 60% or more of store properties are "in play" over a 36-month period due to lease expirations, short-term year-to-year deals, kick outs, and options. Generally, 70% to 80% of deal activity relates to lease renewals.

A well-organized portfolio planning process driven by asset management principals can significantly improve shareholder value.

Distortion of resources is a core financial and asset management principal, but it offends our innate sense of fairness.

It also challenges our mindset about operating as a chain and building a brand. Distorting capital and management resources to flagships and "A" locations means operating those stores differently – management salaries, staffing levels, and technology investments all become elevated. High investments in the best stores leaves older, unproductive, declining locations starved of capital. This distortion flies in opposition to our "every store is a brand representation" mentality. But fortunes are made by asset managers – by divesting poor performing and declining assets and reinvesting money, talent, and technology into top-tier assets. This is a core principle that every stock investor with a portfolio knows works (if only retrospectively).

Let's face it: Many of us would look a heck of a lot better if we lost the 30 pounds we gained since high school - and feel better as well. In the same way, every mature retailer could shed the bottom 20% of their stores and instantly become better looking. While top-line sales will decline, sales per square foot will magically go up, and comp store sales will magically add 100 basis points. Payroll efficiencies, traffic, and conversion per store will improve significantly. The distraction of managing poor performing real estate will diminish, allowing store operations to focus on their best stores. Working capital recaptured will be put to better use. Every metric that investors care about would take an immediate, healthy, positive jump. An even better result would be achieved when those recovered assets – financial and management time – are redeployed to leverage the top 20% of the store fleet and put into other sales generating opportunities including unified customer data management and other omnichannel opportunities.

Jack Welch made GE the best-performing stock for two decades by rigorously applying this principle. As one of his few core principles, it was so important to him that he applied it not only to determine which business he would invest in, but, famously, to his human talent asset pool as well. The Boston Consulting Group (BCG), now one of the top three international business consulting firms, started life touting its four-quadrant matrix for segregating assets into Stars (invest), Dogs (divest), Cash Cows (milk), and Question Marks (grow or divest). Eddie Lampert and his ESL fund are doing a great job of divesting losers – breaking up Sears and selling the pieces that were worth more than the whole. Sears suffers an end-of-life decline, but ESL investors are doing quite nicely.

Simon and other top-tier developers have already applied this principal to their portfolios, spinning off their lower-tier properties and magically boosting the sales-per-square-foot, traffic counts, rental rates, and occupancy metrics.

Yet company resources devoted to optimizing their real estate portfolio assets are often weak and outdated. For most specialty retailers, their core real estate business processes were created during the retailer's growth phase, when monthly deal meetings focused on sexy new stores and new malls – shiny future sources of revenue, drawing the excited attention of senior management. These meetings are poorly structured for approving portfolio lease actions. Mature retailers now need to shift the bulk of their attention and investments towards the far-less-glamorous task of rationalizing existing fleets: what stores to renew, renegotiate, resize, remodel, refresh, relocate, or simply retire. These decisions require entirely different tools and processes.

PROCESS

The first step is admitting you have a problem. If your portfolio lease renewal and capital reinvestment decisions are driven by lease expirations and actioned through monthly real estate meetings, you have a big opportunity to improve decision making. If you have built an analytical approach driven by finance, in partnership with real estate and store operations, you are on the right path. Best-practice retailers make portfolio strategy an annual process, tied to board-level capital budget approval.

Portfolio strategy is a store-by-store plan of action that buckets each store into lease action (renew, renegotiate, resize, remodel, refresh, relocate, or close) and capital investment decisions (relocate, expand, downsize, or remodel "A" "B" or "C" level remodels). A review of past real estate committee decisions will reveal a host of variables that have been used to justify one action or another. The age and condition of each store, quality and performance trends of the center or locale, regional economic trends, competitive intensity, store performance and performance trends, store design, and potential transfer sales or sales erosion from nearby stores and ecommerce all are considerations in segmenting stores for their appropriate slice of the capital pie. Crafting that strategy requires six essential building blocks

Develop Multiple Store Remodel Programs

You need to develop "A", "B", and "C" level refurbishment programs. You cannot distort capital if every store requires a full remodel and the only alternative to full remodels is to do nothing.

Maximize Markets, not Locations

Market strategy starts with understanding who your customer is and where they live in relation to potential store sites and, increasingly, how they shop across your ecommerce and brick-and-mortar channels. Most mature specialty retailers have made significant investments in capturing customer data, often capturing 75% or more at the individual, identifiable customer level.

Of course, raw data needs to be aggregated and analyzed, but understanding your store trade areas based on your customer and understating the interplay between ecommerce and brick-and-mortar, is a relatively cost-effective beginning set of analytics. You can't optimize your real estate portfolio without optimizing markets though proper analytics.

Aggregate Data

Much of the critical information needed to make informed portfolio decisions exists, but is siloed in separate financial, deal, store design and construction, lease admin, marketing, and business intelligence databases. Current store financial performance data is locked in core financial systems. Other store performance indicators, such as traffic and conversion, are kept elsewhere. Store design and construction data, if it exists, is in store-planning spreadsheets or "as built" plans. Customer data is "owned" by the CRM group and closely protected. Lease administration systems are the keepers of key dates and rental obligations. Real estate captures critical information on mall and competitor performance in deal negotiations and the developer portfolio review, typically stored in flat files on FTP sites or handwritten on center lease plans. Real estate executives have great individual knowledge of deals, centers, and markets that needs to be captured and become institutional knowledge. Analysis requires building a real estate attribute dataset.

Adopt Decision Rules

Real estate committee approvals rely on a set of unwritten rules, often applied inconsistently. We recommend explicit rules that will clearly show, for example, what level of store or center or market performance, combined with store conditions and critical-date triggers, are required to justify a full remodel investment versus a partial remodel, or when a 10-year renewal is preferred over a short-term, year-to-year lease extension.

When seven or more variables (store performance, center performance, store condition, store and center trend, transfer or recapture sales impact, store size, store location) potentially impact remodel and lease term decisions, there are nearly an infinite combination of possible decision rules (actually 7*6*5*4*3*2*1 or 5,040).

Retailers often simplify that decision making process by using a variation of the old BCG matrix model, segregating their fleets into winners and losers by some combination of store profitability and mall type ("A" store in "A" locations are planned for full remodel, "B" stores in "A" locations are lower-tier investments, "B" stores in "C" locations are even lower investments with shorter lease terms. Even this simple approach quickly becomes complex, so it usually falls to real estate finance or an equivalent department to build the data sets and develop the first pass "candidate strategy" lease term and capital recommendations.

Validate through Store-by-Store Market Review Meetings

An analytical and financially driven portfolio strategy will generate a candidate action for each store, usually without the benefit of a market overview. To begin the process and build alignment, conduct store-by-store market review meetings. Both the preparation for these meetings and the execution of their outcomes require cross-functional alignment. Finance owns asset management and capital budgeting; the brand owns positioning and customer data; Store Operations contributes valuable market knowledge and lives with these decisions; Real Estate and the market research function bring knowledge on both market positioning and market rents and are responsible for deal execution.

With "all hands-on deck" market review meetings, begin with a market overview and ideal market plans. Renewing five poor-performing, but profitable stores in a three-store market will not likely be the best strategy once everyone understands market dynamics and market optimization. Add the insight that store operations brings on potentially strong but recently poor-performing stores (construction disruption, local economic distress, poor store leadership, etc.). Leverage real estate's knowledge of new competing centers and declining centers that will change the market alignment. Determine the final store-by-store strategy based on all this input to have a definitive market-based portfolio strategy.

Review Annually

Capital budgets change from year to year. Markets are fluid and changing at an accelerated pace with new retail nodes and the consolidation of traditional shopping centers. Millennial lifestyle choices are making big impacts on real estate choices. The growing ecommerce channel and developers' commitments to invest in only their best properties are contributing to a shrinking mall world. Last year's strategies will only be partly implemented, as real estate needs to negotiate with developers who may have other plans and multiple leverage points. Retailers need to monitor and update fleet strategies yearly.

Outcome

Portfolio strategy results in a store-by-store real estate plan that denotes desired lease term, capital, and action (renew, renegotiate, resize, remodel, refresh, relocate, or simply retire).

Benefits

The benefits are substantial and quantifiable:

- Capital and lease term decisions are optimized. Proactive planning helps avoid overspending on suboptimal deals and thus increases the enterprise return on investment.
- The executive leadership team becomes fully aligned through the market-by-market, heads-down review. The board has confidence that the capital budget presented is realistic and based on financial metrics.
- Markets are better planned as portfolio strategy takes into account transfer sales and identifies poorly positioned real estate.
- Real estate execution in general becomes more effective with real estate having a clear plan of action (as opposed to the "bring a deal to committee and we will decide if we like it" approach we see all too often).
- Portfolio negotiations with large multi-property Real Estate Investment Trusts (REITs) become infinitely more productive. Real estate isn't guessing which tradeoffs to make; they have a plan to execute. (See chapter on Managing Landlords)
- Real Estate Committee meetings will be shorter and result in quicker and better reasoned decisions.

8

MULTIPLY OPTIONS

Southwest Airlines only buys Boeing 737 jets, simplifying crew training and ground operations, as well as maximizing flexibility. It is a great economic lesson on the benefits of operating as a chain. Most big-box retailers, from Walmart and Target to Lowes and Home Depot, operate very similar store footprints to obtain chain benefits: uniform floor sets, window displays, staffing models, and a host of other standardized operational models.

This is a bad model for specialty retail, especially if the operating model is based on exclusively operating regional enclosed shopping center stores. Regional enclosed suburban shopping centers, while in many cases still very productive, are losing market share and traffic. In addition, the regional mall landlords do you no favors by driving hard bargains and using their portfolio leverage to their advantage.

Like Lululemon's stores next to yoga studios in urban and suburban high streets, vineyard vines with it resort stores, Kay Jewelers long ago developed Jared, its off-mall alternative and Gap created an entirely different chain and real estate strategy with Old Navy. Many companies have developed value versions of their brands and operate successfully in dedicated outlet centers and are now looking for urban infill locations for their value brands. Restoration Hardware developed its mansion-store concept, whose economics are driven by much lower anchor-store-type occupancy expenses large, for metro-wide trade areas.

Just as Victoria's Secret can open its preferred multi-brand store but can also support separate PINK and Victoria's Secret Beauty stores, dual gender brands may open Men's only or Women's only stores as H&M does, particularly in Europe.

Flagship stores can generate huge sales, and popup stores are the flavor of the day.

The better regional malls, even with the recent declines in traffic, generate the highest average sales per square foot of any real estate category and are also a critical element of market strategy. But nothing creates better real estate negotiating leverage than developing an appetite for multiple alternative real estate venues.

Our chain mentality inhibits us. Different venues require different operating models, from staffing plans to store front and window displays to store prototype design. But the payback in real estate flexibility and negotiating leverage makes it worth it.

"Brand" sometimes incorrectly kills otherwise good real estate opportunities. The phrase, "it's not brand right," seems to stifle all discussion and has killed more opportunities than any other single criteria. Consider awareness of where your customers shop as a balance to brand imperatives. If your customer shops a center, is it really brand wrong? This is especially true in mid- and smaller markets where venues have a more eclectic tenant mix.

9

THE TRUTH ABOUT SALES MODELS

Don't confuse a sales model with either analytics or strategy. A formula-driven calculation generated at the end of a deal process as a requirement for deal approval is not strategy. Running multiple sales models for multiple opportunities in a market is not market planning. The industry standard for sales models is plus or minus 20%, 80% of the time. Companies buy a sales model, often at a significant one-time cost, then find that a year or two later it no longer works and then decide that strategy and analytics are just overblown. They conclude that the "geodemographic nerds" really can't forecast sales any better than the store operations and real estate executives, and then eliminate their entire real estate analytics budget.

Getting markets priorities right and getting portfolio strategy in place is infinitely more critical for real estate success than putting illusory faith in "getting the number right" when approving individual deals. As pointed out in the preface, every deal that comes to real estate committee works and may be validated by a sales model, but that doesn't mean you are working the right deals.

Nevertheless, sales models are an important financial control, often mandated by good corporate governance policies. An impartial, statistically valid projection gives needed pause to "good deals" like the afore mentioned Bee Cave and Hunt Valley examples. They will also compensate for overly conservative sales numbers sometimes proffered by the store operations teams, who are often held accountable for success and thus naturally cautious.

Don't expect last year's model to work for next year's deals; markets change, customers change, and real estate evolves. The model you bought today is based on 18-month-old data points when you were only opening in "A" malls. Now you are opening in "B" malls, lifestyle centers, and street districts – different variables, different models. If you spend money on store forecast models, expect to refresh the model annually.

10

REVIEW, REFRESH

It is not just sales models that become dated quickly.

The Blue Angels perform their aerobatic display over 70 times a year, at times flying wing to wing with only 18 inches of separation. Their flawless execution is no accident. After every single flight, they religiously sit down as a group and critique what went right and what went wrong. They are never perfect but get closer and closer to perfection show after show, year after year, through repetitive analysis.

Real estate analytics is not life or death and nowhere near as close to perfection as the Blue Angels, but it is every much as iterative. The competitive environment retailers operate in moves incredibly fast, as does real estate, so it pays to continuously review and refine base assumptions.

Establish a cadence for regular hindsight on all aspects of real estate, including bottom-line performance of sales and operating-cost assumptions, capital-cost budgets, and execution compared to approved deals, market, and portfolio strategies.

Expect to update market models, growth priorities, portfolio strategies, and sales models annually. You will eliminate many unforced errors and stack the odds in your favor.

11

REAL ESTATE COMMUNICATIONS

In the movie Wall Street, Gordon Gekko values information so highly that he looks everywhere and listens to everyone – even to an ambitious schlub from a Brooklyn phone room. Wall Street pays millions to gain slight information advantages, and their history of straddling ethical boundaries has created an entire regulatory scheme to level the playing field. In response, companies invest in sophisticated corporate communications.

Corporate investment in communication is not merely regulatory window dressing. It exists because clear, controlled, and consistent messaging delivers value.

Clarity: Investors reward clear messages. Clarity around your brand positioning, growth or restructuring initiatives, and financial objectives are rewarded by the stock market.

Controlled messaging: It's critical to speak with one voice and to frame the dialogue in a way that provides maximum benefits. Whether that means understating great quarterly earnings or explaining poor results, the objective usually is to get buy-side and sell-side analysts that cover your industry focused on your brilliant long-term positioning, brand strategy, and future profitability. Analysts who look solely at the shiny object of quarterly results to divine what they mean need to be redirected; you want them focused on how you are **building value** long term.

Consistency: The best messaging is repetitive to the point of tedium. Investor relations is happiest when they can say, quarter after quarter, "these results are consistent with our long-term strategy to deliver shareholder value by" a given date. If your investor relations team could just copy the prior quarterly report and change the date, they would be ecstatic. Wall Street hates risk and variability and rewards consistency.

Clarity, control, and consistency are just as important in real estate. Developers are a key relationship to be nurtured and cared for. They control access to a very important asset needed for success. They are both a partner and an adversary. They reverse engineer, with great accuracy, your P&L to determine how much you can pay and are in the business of maximizing their ROI, not yours. The message you deliver to developers is critical. Yet few retailers have a structured communication program targeting developers.

Enter any random two dozen companies' real estate criteria into a search engine and you will likely find – nothing. J. Crew calls out their social responsibility beliefs, J. Jill points to their Compassion Fund, and Abercrombie & Fitch hypes their Diversity & Inclusion program. But none of those even list a contact number for real estate, much less, actual usable information*.

In lieu of strategic messaging, it is often left to the CFO to craft a "numbers" message for the earnings call, missing an opportunity to use communications to leverage deal negotiations, and sometimes inadvertently putting real estate at a disadvantage.

---

*With no scripted messaging, real estate creates its own message from what they glean in real estate approval meetings or read in the annual report. CEOs and CFOs frequently meet with the heads of the major REITs, talking with authority but without a script, and occasionally that meeting is consumed with short-term tactical venting – a deal gone south, recriminations over unpaid allowances, or a space given to a competitor. The opportunity to reinforce long-term strategy is lost and may undermine the negotiation tactics real estate has carefully employed.

12

COMMUNICATION THAT WORKS

A well-structured real estate communications program, with little cost or effort, can improve deal flow, enhance negotiation leverage, and send a more positive proactive message to investors.

Deal Flow

Even the best real estate strategy needs deal flow to optimize results. Effective real estate is a numbers game: The more opportunities there are available, the more opportunities there are to win. Two suitable deals to fill a market void give obvious negotiating leverage. Three potential deals for one opening are even better. (Hopefully you have followed advice found elsewhere in this book and have developed multiple real estate prototypes that can work equally well in multiple real estate venues: value, high street, community, lifestyle, enclose mall, etc.). Alternatives enhance opportunities, opportunities create negotiating leverage.

Define, then promote, your real estate criteria; make it downloadable from your website. Encourage more ideas at the front end of the pipeline. While you may be afraid that 85,000 commercial brokers will flood you with deals, they are easy to screen if your criteria are crystal clear. Like Gordon Gekko, your team may find an overlooked gem in the process.

Negotiating Leverage and Shareholder Value

Real estate communication benefits go well beyond trolling for opportunities. What you say and how you say it can impact stock price and help or hinder real estate negotiations.

In communicating to the investor community, you are also sending the same message to the developer community. Act as if the large REITs that manage the majority of specialty retail sites are listening to every earnings call and analyzing every annual report. Because they are.

How you deliver your growth message matters. Growth strategy statements need to be more nuanced than "we will open X number of stores per year" or "we plan 5% annual square foot growth." In fact, one large company we did a best practice review for had a stated goal of opening 50 stores per year. And for the four years prior, the real estate team delivered exactly 50 stores. What are the odds that there just happened to be 50 perfect deals four years in a row? Isn't it more likely that in some years that there were 60 deals, and that in some years pricing was just too competitive and there were really only 35 deals? But clearly, corporate communications or inflexible budgeting guidelines drove real estate, and good deals were held back in opportunistic years and poor deals were pushed forward just to hit a number.

Wouldn't it have been better to say (and mean) "we are targeting 3% to 7% long-term square footage growth, depending on availability and price"? Wow! Doesn't that give the real estate team negotiating leverage and isn't that also the best strategy? Wall Street will still build their 5% growth model and calculate their DCF valuations just the same and won't punish you if you are short of a stated number. More importantly, the deal negotiation team gains leverage. There is nothing better in negotiating than having an attitude that implies "I don't need to do this deal."

Communicating asset management (see chapter) plans and results pays dividends. Limited Inc. closed or repurposed 1,000 stores between 1998 and 2001. The closings were accompanied by a positive message, included in the Annual Report Chairman's letter and in numerous meetings with buy-side and sell-side investment analysts, that closings were part of a larger asset-management-driven portfolio strategy to divest poor performers and to reinvest in top performers. It was a good strategy that resonated with investors. The stock price doubled in that three-year period. (Previously, Limited had never purposely closed a store and was being widely admonished by Wall Street for its non-core investments, so this signaled a major change in corporate financial strategy).

Following the 2008 financial crisis, a number of brands announced store closing programs and gave Wall Street a number only – a practice that is widely continued to this day. For example, in 2019 Office Depot announced it was closing 50 stores, and Pier 1 announced it was closing 45 locations following 30 closures in the previous year. Ann Inc. took a different tack in announcing that it, too, was recessing its portfolio to shed unprofitable stores – but without any specific number target. Instead, they went to developers with a more compelling case for rent reductions: Are you in or out? Do you want to be on our close list, or will you work with us and restructure our deal terms? Ann Inc. did a far better job than its competitors during that difficult period. Effective corporate communications put real estate into a better negotiating position.

In the chapter on market pricing, we will discuss the extent to which a company essentially sets their own market price through word and deed. The right communication script delivered by the CEO can be a powerful tool to tamp down developer expectations. Craft messaging that sends a positive message to investors and enhances negotiating leverage.

PROCESS

Involve communications professionals in the messaging.

Set time aside in the Real Estate Committee meeting to brainstorm and develop an appropriate real estate messaging strategy.

Frame the script to maximize negotiating leverage. Avoid putting a collar around real estate with inflexible short-term objectives. Define growth as a multiyear objective and give real estate the latitude to say: "we don't need this deal." Tell both Wall Street and developers what your portfolio strategy is (in general terms), especially fleet size and closings or repositions, to also lay the groundwork for portfolio negotiations. Periodically review financial plans in hindsight or as market changes dictate.

Communicate with consistency and clarity. Write the script so that the CEO, the CFO, the VP Digital, the Chief Merchant, the Chief Store Operator, and the Real Estate Team all repeat the same message.

Establish a cadence. Follow up earnings calls, especially if there is a change in growth or portfolio strategy. After new store openings, thank the developer. If a developer invests tens of millions of dollars in a center upgrade or adds a key tenant that builds traffic, thank them. Be top of mind.

Drive the deal pipeline by casting a wider net with criteria on your website – both to find opportunities and to put developers on notice that you have alternatives.

*Google "Cato real estate criteria" for a best practice example.

13

LEASE LANGUAGE AND LETTER OF INTENT

There is an apocryphal story about a well-known developer that would immediately put the "at risk" label on any store and would start looking for replacements if the new tenant signed their "standard lease."

For new-to-retail, natively digital, and wholesale brands, it is easy to overlook the importance of lease language. Lease language protections are equal in importance to rents. Larger, mature brands have skirmished for decades with developers' attorneys and are on constant alert with regards to their developers' "standard" form leases.

Critical protection language is essential, and it starts at the letter of intent stage:

Kickouts tied to store sales performance are a common tool to protect against failing performance, whether self-inflicted or due to shopping center deterioration. Typically written as a sales-threshold failure – that is, if the store falls below X number of dollars in sales by year three – then the tenant has the right to give notice and terminate the lease with some appropriate advance notice. There is endless discussion regarding what the threshold sales level is, how many years is sufficient, and what constitutes appropriate advance notice.

Radius clauses are often requested by developers and often rejected by tenants. The landlord wants his property protected and having key tenants signed to radius clauses is thought to prevent a competitor from opening a competing center nearby. Retail tenants of course like the flexibility of having no restraints should a better property emerge. Generally, in most categories, and in most centers, retailers have been able to say no to radius restrictions and approve them only on an exception basis.

Co-tenancy clauses have become essential for retailers and a poison pill for REITs. A co-tenancy clause gives retailers the right to pay a reduced rent (typically a percentage of sales in lieu of all charges) if the center falls below a negotiated occupancy or loses one or more key anchor tenants.

Pre-negotiated closing costs. If you sign a ten-year lease and then close the store, you are obligated to pay the entire ten years rent and charges, although in many states the landlord has an obligation to mitigate their damages. If launching a new-to-retail brand, it is advisable to pre-negotiate and limit the closing obligation should you decide to exit the brick-and-mortar strategy.

Relocations clauses. Landlords will frequently ask for the right to relocate your space to a suitable replacement (at their cost). Requests to relocate your store during the term of your lease absent such a clause provides great leverage to accomplish other objectives, so avoid giving relocation rights, especially if you are paying a premium for a desirable center court or other highly visible "A" locations.

Assignment Rights. A landlord will want to restrict your ability to assign the lease under certain merger conditions, and you want free assignment, or consent "not unreasonably withheld." You don't want a developer to hold up an otherwise beneficial business combination.

Sales definition and overage rents. If you are successful, a landlord will want a portion of your profits. One developer is on record saying that the more profitable you are, the higher the percentage of profit that should go to the landlord. Before the internet, sales were those recorded at the store POS system, and a retailer just had to push for standard-deductions language (credit card fees, employee sales, and others). Now, with return to store, order from store, and pickup in store options, developers are arguing for a new definition of sales. Not coincidentally, ICSC, the developers trade organization, is publishing a series of white papers on the halo effect that brick-and-mortar stores have on ecommerce sales – plus 30% per their analysis. As store sales decline and ecommerce sales rise, developers are losing their upside and fighting back. This is the number-one lease language issue, and once new wording finds its way into a lease, it will become a form-lease clause forevermore. Be careful.

Extras are profit centers for landlords. They include everything from inflated fees for insurance, utilities, trash and marketing funds, to the rate for overage rent. It may seem silly to kill a deal over the landlords insistence that the percentage rent should be 8%, when you feel that your sales will never exceed the breakpoint, or to accept a radius clause when you know you will never build a second store close to the first. But in reality, anything you accept will be a starting requirement in all subsequent deals. You need to have the fortitude to draw red lines from the start. Benchmark across landlords and property types and set limits to the best of your ability, for example, by insisting on direct billed utilities.

Absent a change in ownership and leadership, and a willingness to "go to war," you are somewhat locked in by your past acceptance of deal terms.

PROCESS

Hire Experts

There are many experienced and competent real estate attorneys available if deal activity requires an in-house solution due to economies of scale. Third-party individuals and specialist firms that have decades of experience negotiating retail leases can be hired at a cost of between $3,500 and $15,000 per lease. (Negotiating final lease documents when a form lease is in place would represent the lower end of that cost range, while one-off complicated urban deals might fall in the upper end).

Do not hire your existing corporate legal firm unless they have an established real estate lease negotiation practice and years of experience. This is another area in which the big REITs and landlords have established a competitive edge through decades of pushing the envelope.

Use an outside firm to benchmark your language against best practice; while it is difficult to change embedded form lease language, it is worth knowing where you have comparatively strong or weak language. There will come a time when the developer needs something from you; have an arsenal of things to ask for in return.

14

STORE PROTOTYPE

Every retailer has one or more store prototypes. These are highly detailed physical store designs that appropriately translate brand and customer engagement priorities, including differentiated design for pop-ups, flagships, value, and full price.

Creating a new prototype design can be an expensive proposition. We have seen prototype designs developed for less than fifty thousand dollars and for millions of dollars. There are notable design firms around the world, from Tokyo to Paris to Toronto to New York, that will gladly work with CEOs, Chief Marketing Officers, and other C-level executives to create that special look and max out their budgets doing so.

Prototypes may cost two or three times more than a rollout design might cost, as fixtures and other millwork are one-offs or one-of-a-kind, allowing no production economies; GCs will pad their bids for the inevitable change orders and unknowns. Adding to the cost is the tendency to build new prototypes in high-profile locations. If the location is high-profile, then over-the-top design elements are easily justified. Once embedded into a new prototype, those higher-cost design elements just lead to future value engineering problems on roll out to smaller markets or smaller volume stores that can't generate an adequate return on investment.

Unfortunately, the industry is littered with beautiful designs that are too expensive or too impractical to roll out, or that are too ill-conceived for efficient store operations. After the first two or three new prototype stores are built, there is often an immediate effort to value engineer.

PROCESS

We highly recommend that any new prototype design should start with a "cost per square foot" budget objective and the design firm or team should be partnered with a design development team that includes purchasing, finance, and construction expertise. The function of the design development team is to concurrently calculate a detailed cost model by bidding materials, suggest alternatives, review preliminary architectural drawings for feasibility and completeness, and, in general, put guard rails around the process.

Properly structured design development can accelerate time to production and eliminate many costly over-the-top design elements. Concurrently sourcing brand appropriate substitutes will ensure the final design will achieve budgeted build-out cost requirements.

15

MARKET RENT

The first recorded reference to unicorns dates to ancient Babylonia. There are written descriptions in ancient Roman, Greek, Persian, and Jewish texts. There is a medieval cookbook that includes a recipe for cooking the beast. It became the national animal of Scotland in the late 13th century. For most of recorded history, the world believed unicorns to be real, if elusive.

Like the unicorn, the belief in market rent is universal, but finding it is elusive.

Our analytics on thousands of rent data points do show a

correlation with center performance. However, within specific centers, the rents might vary by plus or minus 30%. On a $100 average rent center, that range might be as little as $70 to as high as $130.

There are several factors at work to cause this variability. First, blame Karl Marx – his famous dictum "from each according to his ability, to each according to his needs" has been half adopted by the major REIT developers, who firmly believe "from each according to their ability to pay." The inconvenient truth is that if you are making outstanding profits, then the developers want their share, because, in their minds, you could not be successful if it were not for their benevolence in letting you use their valuable assets. In fact, they are on record asserting that the more profitable you are, the bigger the share of profits due them.

Second, your own behavior sets your market rent. If you consistently demonstrate that you are okay paying 18% occupancy costs in an "A" property (by approving deals, signing leases, and renewing leases with an 18% occupancy cost), then 18% essentially becomes the rent being quoted. And for the big REITs, it will be a short career for any leasing agent that brings in the next deal at 14%. (Yes, they can and do compare all your previous deals and cost of occupancy to the current deal before it is approved by their committee).

Retailers are especially entangled by their own decisions, especially around renewal deals. On a renewal deal, almost everything is known. The developer has reverse engineered your P&L and knows your profit level. They know that adding several percentage points to your occupancy costs is painful, but they also know you will still make money, perhaps with a little capital investment. Walking away from profitable stores is not a good short-term decision. Hence, a 12% deal becomes a 15% deal. A 15% deal becomes an 18% deal. Recognize that by agreeing to thee increases you have raised the bar for all future deals. Accepting the increase means you have reset your occupancy cost benchmark.

Your real estate team cannot solve this problem. They can skirmish, shorten or lengthen terms, negotiate to have short-term allowance money thrown in (see loan sharking chapter), argue that the mall is not really an "A" property, that traffic is down, try to trade off rent reductions in undesirable properties (see Rent Relief chapter), and so on. They can't say no – that is a CEO or CFO decision, and until given the power to say no, they have very real limited negotiating power. No is the most powerful word in any real estate negotiation.

Of course, the ultimate strategy for changing the market rent level you have set is to change CEOs. When a new CEO comes on board, the Real Estate VP can credibly say that 'there's a new sheriff in town,' and what worked in the past won't work in the future. Even then it is a painful process requiring one to turn down deals and close stores on renewal, even if they are marginally profitable, and there is no certainty that the landlords will cave on their future deal economic expectations. We don't recommend firing the CEO to get better negotiating leverage, but if you are a new CEO, understand the enormous one-time leverage to reset the occupancy portion of your economic model.

16

MANAGING LANDLORDS

The major REITs (Real Estate Investment Trust) that control a majority of shopping center and outlet center properties are in the business of making money on their assets – it is their sole reason for existence. They are better at it than the retailers they are negotiating with. Why? For starters, they have a tremendous information advantage.

They know your rents and sales across their properties. Since there has been significant executive movement from one REIT to another, they likely know deals with their (REIT) competitors' rent rolls as well. They know your occupancy cost structure and have reverse engineered your store P&L with remarkable accuracy. They know what you can afford to pay and your "threshold of pain." They listen to earnings calls and know your capital budget and what growth or store closing number you have committed to Wall Street. They know what your competitors pay, where they want to grow, and who could take your space if you back out (few retailers pattern competitors' real estate). They are now working on tracking your omnichannel sales and amending lease language to get better insight into returns and ecommerce sales generated at both your store and in the catchment area of their centers.

Next, they have invested in specific technology to enhance negotiations. They have fingertip ability to view a report comparing a proposed deal to your last dozen deals and all rents across their portfolio. REITs benchmark your entire portfolio whenever a new deal goes to their committee. If you are paying 17% on West Coast real estate, they are not going to approve a 14% deal on the East

Coast. It is unlikely a leasing agent will be able to go backwards on a deal proposed to their deal committee or last long in their job if they do.

Finally, they use their leverage, especially with prime properties and in portfolio negotiations. That sounds like a soft statement, but it is a harsh reality.

Level the Playing Field

Improving management of these relationships is critical to managing occupancy costs. Many of the previous chapters provide clear markers: develop a real estate communications strategy; build market plans and three-year portfolio strategies; watch your form lease language; develop prototypes and operating models and an appetite to operate in multiple venues. But closing the information advantage will be the biggest weapon you can give real estate to improve deal economics.

PROCESS

Most retailers are at a serious information disadvantage. You operate in a world where your negotiating adversary has better actual performance and competitor information, better market intelligence, and more capable technology that puts data at their fingertips.

In addition, whatever data or information a retailer has is often compartmentalized. Store P&Ls, CRM data, store design, store condition, prior approved and disapproved deals, and critical lease dates all reside in their respective organizational silos. Similarly, almost all companies require transaction executives to obtain current competitor sales and center performance benchmarks. This information is locked away in flat files or deal spreadsheets when it could more useful if uploaded to a real estate deal database. Sales model components such as trade area demographics also reside in a separate system, limiting their value for hindsight analysis.

Deal negotiators are typically organized geographically – by market not by developer, so an East Coast negotiator may not be aware of what the West Coast person is agreeing to. Typically, the first opportunity to see what a colleague has negotiated is the deal pre-meeting, which allows for deal comparisons. But that comes very late in the process.

Technology can narrow the information gap. Good real estate executives often have an incredible memory of their prior deals: what spaces they took, what they paid, and how those deals performed. But relying on memory is not a best practice. Memory is selective. What we tend to remember best are outliers – life's best and worst are firmly etched in our consciousness. We also have a recency prejudice. If something bad happened yesterday, we vow to never do it again, even though the "something bad" may have been a simple normal statistical variation. Yet, too often the real estate committee is relying on individual knowledge and memory rather than institutional knowledge – analytics applied to data.

Landlords can easily pull up your entire portfolio, view your actual sales and occupancy costs by total dollars or per square foot, benchmark occupancy as a percentage of sales, and sort by mall classification. Invest in a tool that gives you the same ability. Preparing a simple deal recap of prior deals sorted by mall classification and landlord should not be difficult, and such a comparison should be part of the Real Estate Committee deal meeting package.

Invest in technology that captures the critical real estate and deal information and build deal comparison tools for real estate to use in negotiations and for deal meeting approvals.

17

REAL ESTATE EXECUTIVE COMMITTEE MEETING

The Real Estate Committee deal approval process is universally considered a core corporate governance process, often explicitly required by Sarbanes-Oxley guidelines. Yet Real Estate Committee approval is only the end of a time-consuming deal identification and negotiation process that includes these steps discussed previously:

1. Establish your store model, market strategy, and portfolio strategy framework
2. Understand the dynamics of market rent and landlord relationships; build an effective landlord communications program
3. Establish lease and LOI requirements
4. Close the information gap with developers and build deal recap comparison tools

The Deal Pre-Meeting

For larger retailers with multiple transaction executives, it is common practice for the senior real estate executive to scrub the deal packages and meeting agenda prior to the formal meeting. If deals are primarily done within the major REIT world, deals should be sorted by developer with a deal recap showing past and currently proposed occupancy costs by mall classification. This is the best control point for managing REIT portfolio economics.

The Deal Meeting

Many deal meetings focus on new stores first. New stores are full of hope and promise, glam and glitter – more so if there is a flagship store opportunity. Real estate executives are generally good at "selling the deal" – and are rightly proud of presenting something they bargained hard for over a period of months. This is the fun part of the meeting.

Portfolio deals are relegated to the end of the meeting, and often presented as packages on simple spreadsheets. Unfortunately, portfolio renewal economics can drive future deals and portfolio decisions lock you into or solve a market problem.

Best Practice

The key first question for any deal should be about how it fits the strategy, not about how it will hypothetically perform or what the space looks like.

Order the agenda by market. If market planning is important, the death of market planning occurs the minute those plans are published and put into a binder on a shelf. Every deal should start with a market overview and a map and data table showing all the existing and targeted stores. The data table should highlight existing and targeted stores and their distance from the proposed deal, performance metrics, lease critical dates, and competitors. This makes the market plan live, iterative, and adjustable – not static. As a substitute, retailers often build an annual target list based on market planning, and they work off the list. If a deal coming to committee is on the list, it automatically meets the strategic hurdle.

Only rarely do deals line up perfectly with preferred criteria. Deals are rarely presented that don't meet financial criteria, but often they may miss out on ideal frontage, square footage, co-tenancy or location within a center. It may be an expensive market or a difficult developer driving up store costs. On walking the center or site, store operations may get that "doesn't feel right" vibe. Someone may ask if you can get two dollars off the rent (the answer is yes*). Eyes pour over the lease plan, looking at sight lines, co-tenancy, and sometimes, enviously, at a nearby space that looks available (it isn't).

The committee's job is to balance these misses against the opportunity in front of them. But if you miss including the strategy fit, then you miss the most important factor. Generally, the "B" space in the "A" center or node will be better than the "A" space in a "B" center or node.

Sometimes it's better to wait. But be aware of the cost of lost opportunity in that equation and be cautious of killing deals that are strategically sound yet miss on size or timing, condition of space, or are slightly short of co-tenant representation. Weigh your "feels wrong" observations against what the analytics say; both are important.

It's tempting and efficient to separate portfolio deals from new store deals, and many companies do. We recommend a market approach, so all deals and all upcoming portfolio deals are visible, building a positive loop into market and portfolio plans.

Build a Real Estate Package that Performs

We have seen real estate deal approval packages that are 17 pages and some that are one page. Yours probably needs to be somewhere in between. The package should include:

- Market map with new store target and existing store network and an accompanying table showing lease expirations/renewals and approved portfolio strategy, as well as previously approved deals in process. If co-tenancy is critical, then add key competitors to mapping.
- Deal summary should include both the basic deal economics and a checklist against key lease clauses, such as radius restrictions, recapture rights, co-tenancy protection, kickout language, etc., and a check against approved market and portfolio strategies.
- Letter of Intent to lead the lease negotiation, including non-economic lease clauses (radius, relocation, kick out, co-tenancy, sales definition, etc.)
- Simple pro forma with calculation of projected performance against hurdle rates. I am not a big fan of seeing a page or two of ten-year cash flows included in the deal package; that is finance's job to verify. Build a simple

P&L.
- Construction cost model and landlord requirements (or construction cost pre-vetted by Store Design and Construction, subject to site survey and final design considerations).

Follow Yoda's advice - Do or do not. Avoid approvals with contingencies – it's bad for business. Developers continue to shop your deal until a lease is signed, and the deal team deserves better. Better to kill an approved deal due to subsequent site survey or site visit feedback than to put deals in limbo.

*Can you get another two dollars off the rent? Inconveniently, the answer to this question is frequently yes, which tends to make the real estate committee feel rather shrewd. The unintended consequence of this is that both the developer and the deal maker may consciously or subconsciously just roll this win into the next deal, leaving no net gain, or worse, leaving two dollars on the table for all future deals, knowing that they will have to deal with and manage this behavior. Additionally, If the deal needs to go back through the developer's real estate committee, you could be delayed for three months, losing store open dates that might be worth well more than two dollars in lower rent. Sending the deal negotiator back to ask about hypothetical "looks available" spaces likewise delays approvals, to no one's advantage.

18

CORPORATE FINANCE CONSIDERATIONS: CAPITAL AND DEPRECIATION

Corporate Finance "owns" the capital budget. It is the arbiter of the use of capital. Real estate construction costs and lease obligations are a company's largest use of capital, with obvious impact on cash flow and total company capital structure. The direction provided has an important impact on real estate success.

Finance courses teach us to jealously guard capital. We learn to calculate return on investment as a precursor to approval and are taught in business school finance 101 to rank all investments and approve them in order of return. Every new store deal that goes to real estate committee must pass a company's hurdle-rate threshold (variously expressed as ROI, DCF, NPV, IRR, or simply payback). The threshold calculations are variations of measuring investment returns, expressed as EBITDA, or cash flow, over a specified time period divided by investment. Depreciation is excluded from the calculation, otherwise it would double-count the investment – both as the denominator and in the numerator as annual cash flow. EBITDA is just correct math.

But that calculation does not mean depreciation is in any way free cash to be returned to investors. Depreciation represents a wasting asset that needs to be replaced. Imagine you own a trucking company. Every 40,000 miles or so, the tires wear out. The investment to replace tires could theoretically be put through an IRR model and measured against all other capital investments, but no trucking company does that. They just budget the capital and replace the damn tires.

Store remodel capital is like replacing tires. Just as a trucking company needs to replace its tires every 40,000 miles, physical brick-and-mortar stores do indeed wear out. Most buy-side and sell-side financial analysts assume in their valuation models that depreciation will be spent to refurbish assets, and they will give you no credit for not spending that capital.

So, spend your depreciation, but spend it wisely. As discussed in the Portfolio Strategy chapter, not all children are equal. Develop "A," "B," and "C" refurbishment plans to smartly reinvest depreciation based on the age of the store, store performance, future center performance, and a host of other factors used in developing a portfolio strategy.

19

CORPORATE FINANCE CONSIDERATIONS: TENANT ALLOWANCE

Salary lenders emerged and thrived in the last half of the 19th century, profitably filling a need, but with immorally high interest rates and questionable collection practices. Social reformers battled the industry, and by 1930, almost all states had passed the Uniform Small Loan Law, capping interest rates on small loans at 42%, thereby crippling the industry. The void was filled by organized crime, which recognized an opportunity perfectly matched to their skill sets – usurious loans to desperate people combined with violence as a collection incentive.

Organized crime loan sharking gave way to the modern payday lender industry. Today there are more payday lender store fronts than there are McDonald's. With nominal caps on interest rates limited in many states to not exceed 36% annually, the industry still manages, through various fees and add-ons, to lend money at an annual percentage rate (APR) of 400% or more. Social reformers continue to fight the industry. Reform movements in many states, including Ohio, cap payday lender returns at 40%, yet the industry continues to thrive.

No retailer would borrow from a payday lender. But retailers regularly finance their growth by accepting – even demanding – tenant allowances, which can easily generate a 40% or higher return on investment to the landlord.

Landlords are happy to lend retailers the necessary capital to build their stores. They are repaid by charging higher rents. The typical rule of thumb is they recover the allowance in three years. A $40-per-square-foot deal with a $75-per-square-foot allowance becomes a $65-per-square-foot rent deal. However, that same lease may stay in place for 10 years, with the retailer paying the incremental rent, not just for a 3-year recovery period but for the term of the lease – In raw numbers, $250 over 10 years to get a $75 upfront construction loan. Worse, at the end of the lease term, that base rent plus any annual increase, is now the new starting point for rent negotiations.

On the surface, this seems sensible – borrow from the landlord rather that tapping into traditional bank financing or lines of credit needed to run a seasonal business. Real estate REITs have very efficient capital structures – 90%-debt-to-10%-equity ratio – with additional tax advantages. This structure allows them to borrow on better terms than the typical retail tenant. This makes build-out allowances seem very attractive, especially to cash-strapped growth retailers.

Private equity, which now owns substantial retailer portfolios, also seems to embrace the idea of using the landlord's borrowing capacity to fund store capital.

And to be fair, on the surface, tenant allowances just seems to be free money – an incentive payment to sign a lease. But let's have a reality check: Landlords are not in the business of giving away free money. They know exactly what they are doing and why they benefit. They borrow at the low rates and lend at payday-rate levels.

Not all tenant allowances are bad – there are circumstances in which a tenant allowance does equate to free money. Developers of distressed centers may very well give big incentives to get desirable retailers to locate in their malls. In fact, historically, malls were created by giving the department store anchors free deals. Department store anchor commitments allowed developers to finance the properties and recoup their investments from the small shop tenants (who benefited from the traffic draw of the anchors). I have no insight into Apple real estate deals but suspect they can get pretty much anything they ask for, including full store build-out. Cabela's early growth was funded by extremely generous multi-million-dollar incentive packages to open, literally in the middle of nowhere. A Cabela's flagship yields a retail nexus of hotels, discount stores, restaurants, strip centers, and gas stations that soon follow. The developer recouped their investment in Cabela's though development of adjacent land.

Additionally, if your store produces above-average sales productivity, that will put you into overage rent. The higher base rent created by allowances is effectively offset by lower overage rent due to a higher breakpoint. That is, indeed, smart negotiating. However, for many retailers, tenant allowances will increase rent and they will repay the landlord many times over. Be cautious of directing real estate to prioritize deals based on where they can get the largest allowance (typically less productive, more desperate centers).

Any risk-adverse CFO should be obsessed with lowering fixed costs. The vast majority of retail bankruptcies are simply caused by the intersection of poor short-term performance bumping against high fixed costs. But knowingly adding to fixed costs by trading long-term fixed rent obligations for short-term capital should be a red flag on the deal.

20

CORPORATE FINANCE CONSIDERATIONS: LEVERAGE

Leverage (using debt to replace equity) for operating companies is inherently bad. Leverage creates a fixed-debt obligation, which raises risk. Repayment of debt comes before shareholder distributions, amplifies earning swings, and reduces flexibility. If leverage was good, investors would achieve it themselves without your help, by buying stock on margin. When the company makes that bet, they are betting the company.

In 1990, with modest but stable cash flow and no inherent growth, Ames Department Stores, a Northeast regional discount store chain, borrowed two billion dollars to acquire Zayre, and within months, following a poor Christmas selling season, filed for Chapter 11 bankruptcy, the largest bankruptcy on record at the time. Toys "R" Us filed for bankruptcy in 2018, with five billion dollars in debt, engineered by private equity interests. Debt leverage killed those businesses and many others.

Real estate operating leases look, smell, and act like debt – they are fixed payments in return for use of an asset. Progressive companies like Target have treated them as debt equivalents for decades. Many of the buy-side and sell-side valuation models treat them in that exact way. The Financial Standards Accounting Board has now passed a requirement requiring lease obligations to be listed on the balance sheet as a liability, and billions of dollars of future lease obligations will now be properly reported on the balance sheet of publicly traded companies.

Private equity and activist investors sometimes seem to ignore this reality, with numerous examples of adding leverage to mature retailers, raising their fixed obligations and thus their break-even point. While they can distribute short-term liquidity gains, with a change in the economy or competitive environment, bankruptcy inevitably follows. This is poor financial stewardship. From Ames to Toys "R" Us, it is not Amazon causing bankruptcy; it's leverage.

21

PRO FORMA:
WHAT IT COUNTS, WHAT IT MISSES

My very first boss explained the difference between accountants and financial analysts: one insists on being precisely wrong, the other imprecisely correct. The real estate approval pro forma template falls into the latter category, but it is often interpreted as the former.

Almost every specialty retailer uses a similar store four-wall P&L, measuring net sales, gross margin, store labor, store occupancy, and store "other" (credit card fees, bags and boxes, utilities, maintenance, etc.) to calculate a store net profit before depreciation and taxes – referred to as cash flow or EBITDA.

Pro forma deal-approval templates project cash flow over the life of the lease, making assumptions on sales and expense inflation and creating an NPV, IRR, or DCF calculation of value. If the calculation exceeds the company's hurdle rate, that deal works.

About the only precisely correct number in the pro forma is the negotiated occupancy cost. Sales, as stated earlier, are going to be plus or minus 20% of projection 80% of the time. Sales are the primary driver of cash flow, although there is some actual variability in gross margin, store labor, and other store expenses. Cash flow is the numerator. Store construction costs are the denominator and store design and construction teams often obsess about getting the correct capital budget number. In reality, the store design and construction cost estimate will change as site surveys are completed, design and architectural drawings are finished, GC bids are submitted, and construction with inevitable change orders is complete. The initial construction cost estimate has a plus-or-minus 10%-error rate built in.

The pro forma does not account for overhead costs of district and regional management, market or national advertising programs and other variable warehouse and headquarter expenses. Nor does the traditional four-wall account for ecommerce sales that the store supports, but it penalizes store performance for the labor costs of processing ecommerce returns, or items shipped from the store.

In summary, the store four-wall P&L is a precisely wrong measure of the value of a store. However, most retailers compensate by requiring a high return on investment as calculated by the pro forma. Often a two-year hurdle rate is the benchmark, which translates to a roughly 45% IRR.

I've reviewed thousands of pro forma calculations and built many dozens of templates. It is absolutely the best tool we have for deal approval. If you are constantly stretching sales estimates or minimizing construction cost estimates to make the deal pro forma "work," then that is a big red flag. On the other hand, if a deal otherwise checks all the boxes on market strategy, co-tenancy, size, and visibility, and the team supports it but finance calculates a 2.1-year payback versus a 2.0- year hurdle, approve the deal as an exception.

22

CONCLUSION

W. Edwards Deming, a statistician who worked for the U.S. Census Bureau during the 1930s and the war years, jumped at a chance to go to Japan after the war and teach a willing audience statistical process control – his life's passion. He is idolized in Japan, which annually awards its Deming Prize for innovative applications of his principles. His teaching transformed the auto industry and helped Japan dominate manufacturing for two decades. His principles have now been widely adopted throughout the world. The auto industry, Boeing, General Electric, and a host of others have made Six Sigma implementation and practices one of their core operating disciplines. Improving quality, as Deming asserted, reduces costs.

Deming's teachings helped Toyota kick Ford and GM in the rear end. The US auto giants were operating on the principal that improving quality cost money and that the best way to ensure quality was to inspect end results. Most specialty retailers run real estate like the 1960-era auto companies. The primary control point for real estate is the monthly real estate meeting – inspecting quality at the end of a long process. When three or four out of ten deals miss their promised performance metrics, the most common remedy is to fire the head of real estate.

I hope this book has provided many ideas for improving processes; it is up to management to insist on implementation.

I'll conclude with these rules to live by:

1. Real estate is about finding opportunities within a strategic framework – you need the strategic framework first.
2. Start with the customer – who they are and how they shop; this is critical in our omnichannel world.
3. Strategy is necessarily linked to a demonstrable, proven, and repeatable store model – store size, sales per square foot, labor and occupancy cost percentage, threshold demographics and psychographics, and capital investment – that generates an acceptable ROI. Define and articulate your store model.
4. Market planning is essential and will eliminate many unforced errors.
5. Most retailers spend 80% of their time on new store discussions and 80% of their dollars (including lease obligations) on the existing store fleet. Build a portfolio planning process to manage the right 80%
6. There are no perfect deals, so don't become locked into inflexible parameters. It's the Real Estate Committee's job to balance the tradeoffs.
7. Re-examine your portfolio metrics to account for omni channel revenue and cost impacts.
8. Build a communication strategy to enhance deal flow and leverage deal negotiations.
9. Build tools and data to offset the landlord's information advantage to compete on an even playing field.
10. If new to your CEO, CFO, or SVP Real Estate role, use that one-time opportunity to reset the market.
11. Understand that real estate is a risk management exercise. Create a high-hurdle threshold (two- or three-year payback) to account for the full cost of a store and plan for 8 out of 10 deals hitting the hurdle-rate target.
12. Avoid overloading the deal pipeline with unknowns – new markets, new centers, new wings in centers, a new urban street store program, and other new venues. These are test strategies, risky until proven, not expansion strategies.

The customer today demands omni-channel and successful retailers are reinventing their customer facing practices and technologies to create a unified customer experience. Real estate decision and approvals can no longer be processed on a center by center, deal by deal basis, but must reflect broader market, portfolio and customer engagement strategies. This is the new real estate world.

Embrace change and find success.

ABOUT THE AUTHOR

Steve Morris is the CEO of Asset Strategies Group, LLC. Since 2002, ASG has helped over 120 specialty retailers improve their real estate supply chain with business service solutions that include analytics, deal negotiation, store design and construction, lease administration, and technology. Prior to ASG, Steve was SVP, CFO and CAO of Limited Brand's Real Estate and Store Design and Construction shared service organization and responsible for over $1 billion in annual occupancy expense spend and over $500 million in annual capital spending. A Harvard MBA, Steve brought more than 25 years' experience in finance, strategy and business reinvention roles in leading national retailers prior to co-founding ASG in 2002.

www.ingramcontent.com/pod-product-compliance
Lightning Source LLC
Chambersburg PA
CBHW020605220526
45463CB00006B/2465